TE UNOFFICIAL JOKE BOOK FOR FANS OF HARRY POTTER VOL. 4

BRIAN BOONE

ILLUSTRATED BY AMANDA BRACK

Sky Pony Press
New York

Copyright © 2019 by Hollan Publishing, Inc.

All rights reserved. No part of this book may be reproduced in any manner without the express written consent of the publisher, except in the case of brief excerpts in critical reviews or articles. All inquiries should be addressed to Sky Pony Press, 307 West 36th Street, 11th Floor, New York, NY 10018.

Sky Pony Press books may be purchased in bulk at special discounts for sales promotion, corporate gifts, fund-raising, or educational purposes. Special editions can also be created to specifications. For details, contact the Special Sales Department, Sky Pony Press, 307 West 36th Street, 11th Floor, New York, NY 10018 or info@skyhorsepublishing.com.

Sky Pony® is a registered trademark of Skyhorse Publishing, Inc.®, a Delaware corporation.

Visit our website at www.skyponypress.com.

10 9 8 7 6 5 4 3

Library of Congress Cataloging-in-Publication Data is available on file.

Cover artwork by Amanda Brack and iStockphoto/Shutterstock

Print ISBN: 978-1-5107-4094-5
Ebook ISBN: 978-1-5107-4817-0

Printed in China

Contents

Introduction

What qualities define a Ravenclaw?

First of all they're smart, they're studious, and they're dedicated to pursuing the truth and knowledge in all of its many forms. Not so well-known—but also true—is that Ravenclaws, those bearers of the blue and bronze, are brave, and are unfailingly loyal to their friends and to Hogwarts.

Also, Ravenclaws are funny. Smart people almost always have a great sense of humor, and so we wanted to make this joke book for all the Ravenclaws out there. Not only do we think that a sharp and witty Ravenclaw like you would find *The Unofficial Harry Potter Joke Book: Raucous Jokes and Riddikulus Riddles for Ravenclaws* to be quite "charming," but that it will also cast a spell on you!

But this book isn't just for Ravenclaws. No matter where the Sorting Hat placed you, there's something here for everyone to enjoy, even if you're a Gryffindor or a Hufflepuff . . . or even a Slytherin. (Or even a muggle!) It's full of jokes, riddles, puns, and word games about the people, places, and things that make J.K. Rowling's world of wizards and witches so, well, magical!

So *accio* yourself a comfortable chair, *lumos* that lamp . . . and enjoy!

Chapter 1

LIFE IN RAVENCLAW

Q. So how is life as a Ravenclaw?
A. Pretty Ravenclawsome!

•

Q. Did you hear about the Ravenclaw who went to the Olympics?
A. She won a blue-and-bronze medal!

•

Q. What do you call a wizard who never leaves the library?
A. A Ravenclaw!

•

Q. What do you call a wizard who forgot to go to the Yule Ball because they were too busy studying?
A. A Ravenclaw!

Q. What do you get when you cross a Ravenclaw with a Hufflepuff?

A. A Ravenpuff!

•

Q. How does a Ravenclaw work a boat?

A. They Rowena.

Life in Ravenclaw

Q. What do you call a giant trophy that Ravenclaw never wins?

A. A House Cup.

•

Q. Why did Ravenclaw never win a House Cup?

A. Because it wasn't Gryffindor.

•

Q. What's the house song of Ravenclaw?

A. "Fly Like an Eagle."

•

Q. What do you call a Ravenclaw's dad?

A. Her Raven Pa.

•

Q. Did you hear about the Ravenclaw legacy?

A. Her Ravenclaw mother was so excited she was a ravin' ma!

•

Q. What do you call someone who's *almost* smart enough to get into Ravenclaw?

A. Hermione!

●

Q. How was Ravenclaw Tower built?

A. With a Raven saw.

●

Q. In the Ravenclaw dorms, how are the beds arranged?

A. In Rowenas.

●

Q. Did you hear that they named a body of water after Ms. Lovegood?

A. It was Luna Sea!

●

Q. What does a Ravenclaw bring to a picnic?

A. Ravenslaw.

Life in Ravenclaw

Q. Why did every other Ravenclaw want to be friends with Luna?

A. Because Luna Lovegood.

●

Q. What NFL game would a Ravenclaw have a hard time choosing a team to root for?

A. Eagles vs. Ravens.

●

Q. Who's the sharpest in Ravenclaw?

A. The raven claw!

●

Q. What do you call a daring Ravenclaw?

A. Bravenclaw.

●

Q. What do you call a smooth-faced Ravenclaw?

A. Shavenclaw.

Q. What do you call a thrifty Ravenclaw?

A. Savenclaw.

•

Q. What do you call a Ravenclaw who surfs?

A. Rad-venclaw.

Life in Ravenclaw

Q. What do you call a Ravenclaw who hangs out in cemeteries?

A. Gravenclaw.

•

Q. What do you call a greedy Ravenclaw?

A. Cravenclaw.

•

Q. What do you call a Ravenclaw who lives inside a mountain?

A. Cavenclaw.

•

Q. How many Ravenclaws does it take to change a light bulb?

A. Just one. They stop reading long enough to say "*lumos,*" and then they go back to their book.

•

Q. How many Ravenclaws does it take to change a light bulb?

A. Just one—they quickly use some magic and get it done.

7

Q. Why are Ravenclaws always ready for bed?

A. Because they had to climb that gigantic staircase and now they're very tired!

•

Q. What do you call random students wandering the Hogwarts grounds?

A. Ravenclaws who couldn't figure out the riddle to get into the Ravenclaw common room.

•

Q. Did you hear about the mischievous Ravenclaw with a Time-Turner?

A. They took *every* class.

•

Q. Did you know that lots of Ravenclaws don't graduate?

A. They do so on purpose so they can stick around and use the library.

Life in Ravenclaw

Q. What do you call the last person in the library at night?

A. A Ravenclaw.

Q. Did you hear about the Ravenclaw who fell behind on their school work?

A. They were only two months ahead instead of three.

A Ravenclaw walked into a bar. A metal bar. They hurt their head. They were reading and walking at the same time.

Q. Why did the Sorting Hat get a headache?

A. They had to listen to a potential Ravenclaw's wild and zany thoughts!

11

Q. Did you know there are two Ravenclaw common rooms?

A. The official one, and the library.

●

Q. Where do Ravenclaw musicians like to perform?

A. The House of Blues and Bronze.

●

The other Ravenclaws often wore sunglasses around Luna. She was just so much brighter.

●

Q. What do you call a bunch of wizards who get together and study after school?

A. Ravenclaws.

●

Q. Harry Potter wasn't the only wizard with a scar on his forehead. A fifth year Ravenclaw had one too. Why?

A. She had an *accio*-dent.

Life in Ravenclaw

Q. Why was Harry Potter never going to be a Ravenclaw?

A. He wasn't very logical. Were he a Ravenclaw, he would have grabbed one of his Hogwarts acceptance letters off the floor, instead of trying to catch one flying around in the air!

•

Q. Did Luna go to college after Hogwarts?

A. Yes, to a mooniversity.

•

Q. What does the Grey Lady read in her spare time?

A. Boooooooooks!

•

How to Know You're in Ravenclaw

- If you remind the professor they forgot to assign homework . . . and your classmates thank you.
- When you come to a locked door, you don't knock or try to break it down . . . you just wait for the riddle.

- When you're ready to cut loose on Friday night, you play *two* games of chess.
- You're looking for the logical reasoning behind these jokes.

•

Ravenclaw has WiFi. It's just that the password is the answer to one of the world's hardest riddles, and it will change tomorrow.

•

Q. Slytherin has a lake, but did you know that Ravenclaw has a sea?

A. Luna-sea!

•

Q. What shoes do Ravenclaws prefer?

A. Air Jordans.

•

Q. What do Ravenclaws do at the salon?

A. Get air-cuts.

Life in Ravenclaw

Q. What do you call someone who was almost a Ravenclaw?

A. A Ravenclawwwww, so sorry!

•

Q. Why was the Ravenclaw distraught at the end of the semester?

A. They didn't make the grade.

•

Professor: I hope your essay is coming along.
Ravenclaw: It will be when I start on it.

•

Q. What cheese do Ravenclaws prefer?

A. Bleu and bronze cheese.

•

Q. Did you hear that a Ravenclaw found a genie and asked for a wish?

A. They wished for an eighth year at Hogwarts.

Q. What's black and white and read all over?

A. An old picture of some Ravenclaws.

•

Q. Why was the Ravenclaw so sad?

A. They got sick and had to skip classes for a day.

•

Ravenclaw #1: Did you hear that the really smart student got placed into Hufflepuff?

Ravenclaw #2: Nothing of the sort!

•

Q. What do Ravenclaws eat that's cheap and quick?

A. Top Raven.

•

Luna: I'm glad I'm named Luna Lovegood.

Neville: Why is that?

Luna: Because that's what everybody calls me.

Q. What do you get when you cross a fish with a notable Ravenclaw?

A. Tuna Lovegood.

Q. Why did Luna turn her back to the mirror of Erised?

A. She didn't have anything she needed to wish for that day.

•

Q. What does a true Ravenclaw do first thing each morning?

A. They wake up!

Q. Why does Luna's hat help her in school?

A. It helps her get right to the point!

•

Q. How do you know you're a Ravenclaw?

A. If you read this entire book in one sitting!

Chapter 2

Q. Why couldn't the Hogwarts student cheat on a Charms exam?

A. Because the professor put an Anti-Cheating Spell on it!

•

Q. As far as Professor Flitwick's class is concerned, what is Hogwarts?

A. Charm school!

•

Q. What's a good end of semester present for Professor Flitwick?

A. A charm bracelet.

•

Q. What would you get if Professor Flitwick faced Nagini?

A. A snake charmer!

Q. And where would that place Nagini?

A. In charm's way!

•

Q. Did you hear about the student who failed Charms?

A. No charm done!

•

Q. What's Professor Flitwick's favorite snack?

A. Charms lollipops.

•

Q. Who is Professor Flitwick to that special someone?

A. Prince Charming!

•

Q. How did the seventh year Charms student get all the classes she wanted?

A. She charmed her way in.

How Charming!

Q. What do you get when you cross a sea creature with a Softening Charm?

A. *Spongify Squarepants.*

•

Say what you will about *diffindo,* but as far as spells go, that severing charm really cuts deep.

•

Q. How did the girls finally get the boys to dance at the Yule Ball?

A. *Tarantallegra!*

•

Thank goodness Hermione cast a *skurge* spell after the ghosts ran through. And just in slime!

•

All the wizards had a fondness for the student who could do *expelliarmus.*

He was just so disarming!

When Fleur cast an Engorgement Charm on Bill Weasley's heart, that's when he cast an Engagement Charm.

•

Ron: You used an *immobulus*?
Harry: Yeah, a Freezing Charm.
Ron: That's cold!

Q. What did the not-so-smart wizard use to make ice cream?
A. A Freezing Charm.

•

Q. What charm do wizard police use?
A. A "Freeze!" Charm.

How Charming!

Q. What charm do wizard campers like best?
A. *Incendio*, because it's a lot easier than rubbing two sticks
   together.

•

I like the Knock-Back Jinx.
I really *flipendo* for it!

•

Hermione: Does the Memory Charm make you forget?
Luna: I can't remember!

•

Ever since they cast the *Petrificus Totalus* curse
   on me, it really put me in a bind!

•

Ron: She cast *Rictusempra* on me!
Harry: The Tickling Charm?
Ron: Yeah!
Harry: That's hilarious!

Q. What kind of spells do they teach in Intro to Charms?
A. Really basic ones!

•

Q. How do you fix a broken marine animal?
A. *Octopus reparum*!

•

Q. What do you get when you cross peanuts, popcorn, and magic?
A. Cracker Jinx!

•

Q. How does a wizard make a soda fly?
A. *Wingardium levysoda!*

How Charming!

Q. How does a wizard make a butterbeer float?

A. *Wingardium leviosabutterbeer*!

•

Q. How do young wizards make their swings go higher?

A. *Swingardium leviosa*!

The Shrinking Charm just isn't as big as it used to be.

Q. What's the greatest charm of all?

A. Cheering Charm, Cheering Charm, rah rah rah!

Nothing brings a couple of wizards closer than a good *lumos duo* spell.

How Charming!

Depulso was a good charm, but then it had to be banished!

•

Q. Have you ever seen a *stupefy* spell cast?
A. It's absolutely stunning!

•

Wizard #1: Did you hear about the Silencing Charm?
Wizard #2: Ssh!

•

Q. Where did Professor Flitwick learn all that he knows?
A. On a charm farm.

•

Q. What's Professor Flitwick's favorite TV show?
A. *Southern Charm.*

•

Q. How does Professor Flitwick cast spells?
A. With his charmin' arm.

Q. What do wizards use to clean up mishaps in charms class?

A. Charm n' Hammer.

●

Q. What sweet treat should wizards never eat?

A. Bewitched Snowballs.

●

Q. What does a wizard do when they spill butterbeer?

A. They use a Spill Spell.

●

Professor Flitwick: Harry, why is the classroom full of water? Did you use a Water Spell?

Harry: I didn't *aquamenti* do that.

●

Q. In what part of school is *lumos* learned?

A. Glow and Tell!

How Charming!

Q. How would you make a toy hippo appear?

A. *Bogus hippopotamus!*

•

Q. How do you make your patronus appear, but with a bag over its head so nobody knows it's yours?

A. *Expecto patronum anonymous!*

•

Q. How do you make a banjo appear?

A. *Accio banjo!*

•

Q. How can you force someone to give you a holiday gift?

A. *Expelliarmus Christmas presentus!*

•

Q. How do you make salt fly?

A. *Wingardium leviosalt!*

Q. How do you explode a light bulb?
A. *Lumos boomos!*

•

Q. How do you make someone drop their platypus?
A. *Expelliarmus platypus!*

•

Q. How do you get your patronus to eat?
A. *Expecto patronom-nom-nom!*

•

Q. How can you make yourself think really hard?
A. *Expectum cranium!*

•

Q. How do you make an eel appear?
A. *Alohomoray!*

•

Q. How do you make s'mores with magic?
A. *Alohosm'ore-a!*

How Charming!

Q. Did you hear about the wizard who had a wacky day?

A. He intoned *adventurous riddikulus*!

•

Q. What spell should you use to make a dog appear?

A. *Abracadabralabrador!*

•

Q. What spell should you use to make a dinosaur appear?

A. *Tyrannosaurus Hex.*

Hermione: I've been casting spells since I was five years old.
Luna: You must be very tired.

•

Q. Why did Luna always get what she wanted?
A. Because she always said the magic words!

•

Q. Can owls see at night?
A. Sure, but they have a hard time getting out that *lumos* spell.

•

Draco: Sorry I didn't finish my homework, I got hit with an Obliviate Charm.
Snape: How long ago did that happen?
Draco: How long ago did what happen?

•

Q. How do you make a whale fly?
A. *Wingardium levi-orca*

How Charming!

Q. How do you make fried vegetables fly?

A. *Wingardium levi-okra!*

•

Q. What do you do when your flying car won't work?

A. You call a car *reparo* place.

•

Q. How do witches make guacamole?

A. *Avocada Kedavra!*

•

Q. How do you make jeans fly?

A. *Wingardium levis-osa!*

•

Q. What kind of joke is so bad it will kill a wizard's wand?

A. A *nox-nox* joke!

Q. Did you hear about the dumb wizard who tried to disarm another wizard's wand but turned it into salmon instead?

A. He used the *lox* spell, not the *nox* spell.

•

Q. Where are all the bad wands hidden?

A. At Fort Nox.

•

Q. What spell does Harry cast when he's nervous and just wants the mood to lift?

A. *Wingardium nerviosa!*

•

Q. How does a wizard stave off a dinosaur?

A. *Expalliarmus tyrannosaurus!*

•

Q. How do wizards get Filch off your tail?

A. *Argus riddikulus!*

How Charming!

Q. What's a wizard's favorite sci-fi movie?
A. *Wingardiums of the Galaxy.*

•

Q. Did you hear about the wizard who had two spirit guides?
A. He had a bonus patronus!

•

Q. How does a wizard track athlete perform?
A. They shout *discus projectus!*

•

Q. How does the Ministry of Magic balance the budget?
A. With Transfiguration.

•

Q. Did you hear they introduced human anatomy at Hogwarts?
A. The first spell students learn is *abra cadaver.*

Q. What do you get if you cross a rock star and an unforgivable curse?

A. Avada Kedavril Lavigne.

●

Did you hear about the toddler wizard who injured her parents? She was trying to blow bubbles with her wand but said "baubillious" instead, and a bolt of lightning shot out of her wand.

●

Q. How can you tell if you've got a lazy professor?

A. They write on the blackboard with a Blackboard Writing spell.

●

Q. Why does Hogwarts have the best cheerleaders?

A. Because they can use a Cheering Charm.

●

Q. What do wizards chant in the stands at sporting events!

A. Defensive Charms!

How Charming!

Q. Why did Fred and George get kicked out of Divination class?

A. They brought in a magic 8-ball.

•

Q. How do the Weird Sisters prepare for a concert?

A. They cast an Amplifying Charm!

•

Q. What did Hagrid, keeper of the keys, do when he forgot his keys?

A. He just cast an *alohomora* charm!

•

Q. Why is there no climate change in the wizarding world?

A. Because they can just use an Atmospheric Charm.

•

Q. What does Harry Potter use to clean his bathroom?

A. *Scrubbus toiletous!*

Q. What spell goes great on hot dogs?
A. *Relishio!*

•

Q. How do you make yogurt fly?
A. *Lacto levioso!*

•

Q. What are the most enlightening charms?
A. Levitation Charms!

•

Q. How do you transform anything into a joke book?
A. *Jokus riddikulus!*

Chapter 3

Q. What's the worst kind of greeting in the wizarding world?

A. The Deathly Hellos!

•

Q. What's the silliest place in the wizarding world?

A. Riddle Manor.

•

Q. Who makes the worst pizza?

A. Hagrid's Hut.

•

Q. What do you get when you cross Voldemort with Harry Potter?

A. Dead!

Q. Why do Death Eaters wear black?

A. Because Voldemort told them to.

•

Q. How can you tell someone is a Death Eater?

A. If they have a snake and a skull tattoo.

•

Q. Why is the Death Eater tattoo a skull and a snake?

A. Because a bunny would look *ridiculous*.

•

Q. Why did the werewolf cross the road?

A. Because it wanted to.

•

Q. How do you confuse a troll?

A. It's easy: Speak in complete and total nonsense! (It works for non-trolls, too!)

A Trip Around the Wizarding World

Here's your riddle for the day:
Tom.

●

Q. Why is it terrible to get a cold in the wizarding world?
A. It makes your nose full of boggarts.

●

Q. Who's the clumsiest Minister of Magic of all time?
A. Doofus Scrimgeour.

●

Q. What happened to Voldemort's nose?
A. He got a cold and it started running.

●

Q. Why did they call it the Shrieking Shack?
A. Because it shrieked!

●

Q. What do you call Tom Riddle when he's doing laundry?
A. Lord Foldamort!

Q. What do you call Tom Riddle when he's writing in thick letters?

A. Lord Boldamort!

•

Q. What do you call Tom Riddle when he's on ice?

A. Lord Coldamort!

•

Q. What do you call Tom Riddle when he's covered in old cheese?

A. Lord Moldamort!

•

Q. What do you call Tom Riddle when he's been canned by a fruit company?

A. Lord Dole-damort!

•

Q. What do you call Tom Riddle when he's been gilded?

A. Lord Goldamort!

Q. What do you call Tom Riddle when he's vaulting in the Olympics?

A. Lord Poledamort.

•

Q. Who's the resident poltergeist at the French magic school?

A. Boo-Buttons . . . at Beauxbatons.

•

Q. How is Voldemort like Santa?

A. He always leaves something valuable behind!

•

Q. Why was Voldemort comfortable walking around in old, broken-down shoes?

A. Because they had split soles.

•

Q. What dark wizard made the best pancakes?

A. Tom Griddle.

Q. What happens when you cross dessert in the Great Hall with a powerful Death Eater?

A. Luscious Malfoy.

•

Q. What did one wizard friend say to the other?

A. "You're the wand beneath my wings!"

•

Firenze: Why were my kind and I never admitted into Hogwarts?

Dumbledore: We centaur letters, but we never heard back from you.

•

Q. Did you hear about the school for wizard farmers?

A. Instead of house ghosts, they have house goats.

44

A Trip Around the Wizarding World

Q. How do wizards make chicken?
A. They petri-fry it!

•

Q. How did the really handsome wizard survive an Avada Kedavra?
A. Because he was drop-dead gorgeous!

•

Q. How do Dementors drink milkshakes?
A. They suck them out through straws.

45

Q. What did one broken bone say to the other?

A. "Come on, let's Skele-Gro!"

•

Q. What happens if you cross a phoenix and an Aguamenti?

A. A mess!

•

Q. Where did the super-hip Dark Lord move?

A. Voldemortland, Oregon.

•

Q. Did you hear the Dark Lord kept losing more and more of his hair?

A. They started to call him Baldy-More.

•

Q. Did you hear Lucius Malfoy opened a photography studio?

A. He just loved to frame people.

A Trip Around the Wizarding World

Q. What's Voldemort's favorite video game?
A. *Mortal Combat.*

•

Voldemort gave away all his old R&B albums.
He needed to split up his soul.

•

Q. How does Voldemort like his coffee?
A. Black.

•

Q. Why did the animagi buy Spanx?
A. He was looking for something to shift his shape.

•

A prisoner at Azkaban ran right into a Dementor.
He said, "Pardon me."

•

Q. What food are they tired of at Azkaban?
A. Lox.

Q. Did you know they make breath-freshening candy at Azkaban?

A. At least the De-mint-ors do.

•

Q. Did you know they make coins at Azbakan?

A. At least the De-mint-ors do.

•

It's hard to communicate with prisoners in Azbakan. Although they do have cell phones.

•

A prisoner at Azkaban came down with a bad case of acne and they gave her lots of medication.
They didn't want her to break out.

48

A Trip Around the Wizarding World

Q. What do Hogsmeade and Azkaban have in common?
A. Bars.

•

Q. Where can you buy chocolate boxing gloves?
A. At Honey-duke-it-out.

•

Q. Where can you can buy vomit-flavored Bertie Botts Beans?
A. At Honeypukes.

•

Before he made wands, he made his living stuffing pimentos into green fruits.
That's why his name is Mr. Olive-handler.

•

Q. Where does a wizard rest their cup of tea?
A. On their sorcerer.

Q. What's an animagi's favorite movie?

A. *Transformers.*

•

Q. When is a rat not a rat?

A. When it's Peter Pettigrew.

•

Q. Did you know that Ron's rat used to be much smaller?

A. Pettigrew.

•

Q. What Lewis Carroll book do wizards like?

A. *Alice in Wand-a-Land.*

•

Q. Did you hear about the wizard who got lost?

A. He went in the Forbidden Forest and wand-ered.

A Trip Around the Wizarding World

The Weird Sisters couldn't replicate the success of their first
   song.
They were ultimately a one-hit-wand-er.

•

Q. Did you hear about the city where Peeves grew up?
A. It's a ghost town!

•

Q. What's a good name for a witch?
A. Wanda.

•

Q. What's a wizard's favorite film epic?
A. *Gone with the Wand.*

•

Wizards only eat organic food.
That helps them to be supernatural.

If you ever find yourself in the Forbidden Forest, make like a tree and leave.

•

Q. Who has blood type ½-O-Postive?
A. The Half-Blood Prince.

•

Q. Where do you relieve yourself in the Forbidden Forest?
A. In the bat room.

•

Q. What's Voldemort's favorite painting?
A. *The Scream*.

•

Q. Why don't werewolves attack Muggles?
A. They taste terrible!

52

Q. Did you hear that Aunt Petunia's sister went to America?

A. Guess she wasn't a No-Marge!

•

Malfoy wasn't allowed in Gringotts.
There was just no accounting for him.

•

Q. Did you hear Gringotts fired half its goblins?

A. They kept coming up short.

•

They say there's a moat around Gringotts.
It's filled with loan sharks.

•

Q. Did you hear about the goblin who didn't want to work at the other wizard banks?

A. He lacked interest.

53

Q. Did you hear about the goblin who couldn't work at Gringotts?

A. He had a knut allergy.

•

Q. What did Griphook say when Gringotts was robbed?

A. "Well, it's not my vault."

•

Hogwarts didn't have an account at Gringotts because they had no principal.

(Only a headmaster.)

•

Q. Why don't vampires go to Gringotts?

A. They prefer blood banks.

•

Q. Did you hear about the former hat-maker?

A. She was well-qualified to be Hogwarts' headmaster.

54

A Trip Around the Wizarding World

Malfoy nearly crashed his father's fancy car.
Fortunately, the Mercedes didn't break—the Mercedes Benz.

•

Q. Why does Voldemort look like that?
A. Nobody nose!

•

Q. What's Voldemort's favorite kind of comics?
A. Marvolo Comics.

•

Q. What do you get when you cross a blasting curse with a wizard pub?
A. Three Boomsticks!

•

Q. What should you call the Dark Lord's wife?
A. "She who must not be named."

Q. How does Harry get his food out of the oven?
A. With Harry's Potholder.

•

Q. What does Voldemort take for his seasonal allergies?
A. Anti-hissstamines.

•

Before they figured out he was Tom Riddle,
the idea was that nobody nose who
Voldemort was.

•

Q. How do goblins buy milk?
A. By the galleon.

•

Q. What's the best way to cook leeks?
A. In a leeky cauldron.

Q. What do Ron dribbling water and a wizard pub have in common?

A. One's leaky, called Ron; the other is the Leaky Cauldron.

•

There's a condition among wizards in which some can turn into dogs.

And yes, it's Sirius.

Say what you will about the dark Lord, but at least he isn't nosey.

(He can't be!)

57

Q. What's the difference between an old cartoon cat and mouse, and the main rivalry in the wizarding world?

A. One is Tom and Jerry, and the other is Tom and Harry.

•

Voldemort has no nose.
So you know what that means.
He smells horrible!

•

Q. What's it called when you assemble all the horcruxes?

A. A wholecrux!

•

Q. What do dark lords eat for breakfast?

A. Cinnamon Horcrunch.

•

Q. Why did James and Lily Potter regret using Wormtail for their secret keeper?

A. He totally ratted them out!

Q. What does Dobby read?
A. Elf-help books

•

Q. What do wizards call the game of tag?
A. A witch hunt.

•

Q. What's a wizard's favorite reggae band?
A. Magic!

•

Q. What's worse than finding a worm in your apple?
A. The Wizarding Wars.

•

Q. Where do ghosts go to relax?
A. The Boo-Hamas.

•

Q. Where does a dark wizard buy all their supplies?
A. At Volde-Mart.

Q. What do you get when you cross a bony face with the Weasleys' only daughter?

A. Chinny Weasley.

•

Q. Did you hear that Dudley Dursley took up surfing?

A. Everybody calls him Dudely Dursley now.

•

Q. What if the Weasleys didn't have such a big family?

A. Then they'd be the Measleys.

•

The Minister of Magic stopped eating almonds and cashews. Some people prefer their Fudge without nuts.

•

Q. How does Dobby go into a room?

A. By turning the knobby.

•

Q. How do wizards tell time?

A. With a wrist witch.

Let's all give Peter Pettigrew a hand.
He needs one.

•

Q. Who's the most royal of all Harry Potter characters?
A. Kingsley Shacklebolt.

•

Q. How did they know the flying car belonged to Arthur Weasley?
A. The "I Love Muggles" bumper sticker!

•

Q. What do you call it when a baby Dementor crawls?
A. A little creepy!

Q. Why do Inferi move so slowly?
A. They're dead tired.

●

Q. Do Inferi ever rest?
A. Of corpse they don't!

●

Q. Why doesn't anybody want to have a dinner party with Dementors?
A. They're presence is just so draining.

●

Q. When's the most magical time of the year for wizards?
A. All of the time!

●

The *Harry Potter* phenomenon will probably live on for years.
It just keeps Rowling along.

Chapter 4

Q. Why couldn't the quidditch player compete?

A. He had a snitch in his side.

•

Q. Why are quidditch matches played on Saturdays?

A. The goals don't work the next day—because there's no post on Sundays.

•

Q. What do quidditch players say when they find a valuable object?

A. "Seekers, Keepers!"

•

Q. Did you hear a Ravenclaw quidditch player crashed?

A. She was busy reading a book about quidditch.

Q. What did the aggressive quidditch player say?
A. "Comet me, bro!"

•

Q. What quidditch players go on to work at zoos?
A. The keepers.

•

Q. What's a difference between a bad quidditch player and a sleazy politician?
A. One is an awful quaffler, and the other is an unlawful waffler.

•

Q. What quidditch players drink the most butterbeer?
A. Quafflers.

•

Q. What happens when you let chickens play quidditch?
A. You get a lot of fowl balls.

The Quidditch Pitch

Q. What does a tattle-telling Draco and the most elusive element of quidditch have in common?

A. They're a couple of golden snitches!

•

Q. What quidditch players play the drums?

A. Beaters.

Q. Why did Professor Trelawney make a terrible quidditch coach?

A. She used crystal balls.

•

Q. What do you call a bunch of wizards who practice quidditch after school?

A. A team!

•

Q. What broomstick is best for a cloudy day of quidditch?

A. A Nimbus 2000.

•

After Oliver Wood lost his broom, the rest of the quidditch team gave him the brush off.

•

Q. What don't they have at Three Broomsticks?

A. A very good quidditch team!

The Quidditch Pitch

The best-of-seven quidditch final ended with one team
winning the first four games.
It was a sweep!

•

Q. Why do wizards like quidditch so much?
A. It just "sticks" with them.

•

Q. Is quidditch fun?
A. Sure, it's a ball!

•

Quidditch is a lot more popular than it used to be.
In fact, it's sweeping the nation!

•

**Q. Did you hear that the quidditch player got some great
new sneakers?**
A. They gave her a lot of air.

•

Q. Where does a traveling quidditch player stay?
A. In a broom with a view.

Q. Did you hear about the ghost that joined the quidditch team?

A. It played ghoulkeeper.

Q. What do quidditch players say to their brooms at night?

A. "Sweep tight!"

The Quidditch Pitch

Q. When do quidditch players wear armor?
A. For knight games.

Are Pokémon just golden snitches? Think about it—it's a ball
with a magical creature inside that everybody wants to catch!

•

Q. Did you hear the recap of the quidditch game?
A. It was a tall tale!

•

Q. Why is quidditch played on broomsticks?
A. Because it would be boring on foot.

Q. Why is quidditch played on broomsticks?

A. Because the players are too lazy to walk.

•

Q. Why is quidditch played on broomsticks?

A. If they used vacuum cleaners, they'd get all the cords tangled.

The Quidditch Pitch

Q. Why is quidditch played on broomsticks?
A. Because if they did it on horses, it would be polo.

•

Q. How long does a person play quidditch?
A. Until they quid it.

•

Q. How much do professional British quidditch players earn?
A. Lots of quid!

•

Q. What do you get when you cross quidditch with a sea creature?
A. Squidditch!

•

Q. Did you know that there's a junior version of quidditch?
A. Kidditch!

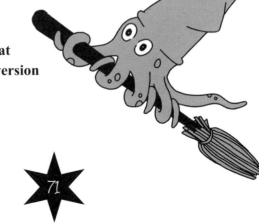

Q. What goes on top of the box where they keep the Golden Snitch?

A. The lidditch.

•

Q. What does a snitch in time save?

A. Nine!

•

Q. What do you call house ghosts that watch quidditch matches?

A. Spook-tators!

Q. Did you hear that Hermione lost her Time-Turner at a quidditch match?

A. Time flies when you're having fun!

•

Q. Why was the quidditch broom confused?

A. It couldn't tell which witch was which!

Chapter 5

Q. Why were the first-years afraid of the Hogwarts ghosts?

A. Because they weren't all there.

•

Q. What's the difference between Gilderoy Lockhart and Grawp?

A. One founded the Dueling Club and the other could start the Drooling Club.

•

Q. Did you know that Peeves wrote his own memoir?

A. He was his *own* ghostwriter!

•

Q. Why doesn't Hogwarts have a basketball team?

A. Because Ron has all the jumpers.

Q. How do teen wizards clean their skin?
A. With witch hazel!

•

Q. How are Slytherins like cards?
A. They travel in packs.

•

Q. Why didn't Mad-Eye Moody see Ron and Harry goofing off?
A. He had a blind spot.

•

Q. What's the best part about having ghosts at Hogwarts?
A. They put the whole place in high spirits!

•

Q. What's a magical place covered in pricklies?
A. Hedgehogwarts!

Q. Why did they call it the Yule Ball?

A. Because Yule be sorry if you don't go!

●

Q. What did Harry have for lunch when he was underwater during the Triwizard Tournament?

A. A sub.

●

Q. Why did Dumbledore throw water on his phoenix?

A. It needed to blow off some steam.

Poor Moaning Myrtle.
She only wanted Harry Potter to be her boo!

•

Q. What does Moaning Myrtle wear when she wants to look fancy?

A. She puts a boo in her hair.

•

Q. What do you get when you cross a bathroom ghost with a tortoise?

A. Moaning Turtle.

House ghosts must be so lonely.
After all, they've got no body.

•

Q. What do house ghosts wear on their feet?
A. Boo-ts.

•

Hermione: Why did you do so poorly on your test?
Ron: Maybe I got hit with a *stupefy*?
Hermione: That's not how that spell works.
Ron: I know, I got that question wrong on the test!

•

Q. How do you get down from the roof of Hogwarts?
A. You don't. You get down from a goose.

•

Q. Why did Nearly Neadless Nick like to celebrate birthdays?
A. He always had presence.

Q. What room is full of questions?

A. The Room of Inquirement.

•

Q. What room is full of wizards with bad breath?

A. The Room of Require Mints.

•

Q. What do you get when you cross a Defense Against the Dark Arts teacher with a tragic movie?

A. Sad Eye Moody.

•

Q. What do you get when you cross a Defense Against the Dark Arts teacher with a skateboard?

A. Rad Eye Moody.

•

A Slytherin couple got into an argument.
But then they hissed and made up.

Q. What do you get when you cross Harry's best friend with itchy red spots?

A. Ron Measleys.

•

Q. What do you get when you cross a bird with the head of Gryffindor?

A. Professor McGonagull.

•

Q. What do you get when you cross a bathroom ghost with the most famous portrait of all time?

A. *The Moaning Lisa.*

•

Q. What happened when Lupin swallowed a clock while he was in werewolf form?

A. He got ticks!

•

Q. What would you get if you gave Professor Lupin some Floo Powder?

A. You'd get a where-wolf.

Around Hogwarts

Q. What would happen if you gave Professor Lupin a Time-Turner?

A. You'd get a when-wolf.

•

Q. Where wouldn't Neville like to visit?

A. The Petrified Forest.

•

Q. What video game is popular at Hogwarts?

A. The Nintendo Witch.

•

Q. Who drew all those haunted paintings in Hogwarts?

A. Vincent Van Ghost!

•

Q. What would you get if you gave Grawp a pogo stick?

A. Big holes in the ground.

Q. Why is the Chamber of Secrets underground?

A. Because it can't climb trees!

•

Q. Why was Filch wandering the grounds in his pajamas?

A. He was on the nightie shift.

•

Q. Why are there no zebras at Hogwarts?

A. They missed the Hogwarts express.

•

Professor Binns: Why did you fail your History of Magic test?
Ron: All that stuff happened before I was born!

Q. What contest do they have at Hogwarts?

A. A spelling bee!

•

Q. Are mummies allowed at Hogwarts?

A. No, they wouldn't be caught dead there!

Around Hogwarts

Harry: What marks did you get in your introductory quidditch class?

Ginny: Plenty! Bruises, too.

•

Q. How were Harry's marks in his Gillyweed training class?

A. Below C-level.

•

Q. What's the difference between a teacher and the Hogwarts Express?

A. The teacher says "spit out your gum!", but the train says "choo-choo!"

•

Neville: I can't figure out this assignment.

Snape: What? Any five-year-old could do it.

Neville: Yeah, but I'm 13!

•

Q. Why did Hermione wear sunglasses to class?

A. Because she was very bright.

After her magical math class, Ginny got lost.
So Ron was centimeter.

•

Q. What magazine does Professor Sprout read?
A. *Weeder's Digest.*

•

Q. Where is the Great Lake the deepest?
A. At the bottom!

•

Ginny: How was Divination class?
Luna: Divine!

•

Q. What's the best thing to find with the Marauder's Map?
A. Marauders!

•

Q. What's a cat at Hogwarts?
A. A hairy purrer!

Q. What's another name for walking around while holding a wand?

A. Wandering!

•

McGonagall: I hope I didn't see you looking at Harry's paper.

Ron: I hope so, too.

•

Q. Who *should* be the Hogwarts Herbology professor?

A. Professor Tree-Lawny.

•

Q. What's another name for graffiti in the Hogwarts bathrooms?

A. Bogg-art!

•

Q. What happens when you cross Hogwarts with severe weather?

A. You'd have a school for blizzards!

Q. Does Severus own a smartphone?
A. Yes, he loves taking Snapes.

•

Professor Sprout handed Hermione a bunch of prickly roses.
"Ouch!" Hermione said.
"Points, Gryffindor!" Professor Sprout replied.

•

The Slytherin bathrooms are always stocked with hissss and herssss towels.

•

Tom Riddle looked great in his Slytherin robes.
Positively Marvelous!

•

Harry did great in the underwater leg of the Triwizard Tournament.
He really made a splash!
Although when he was underwater . . .
. . . he got in trouble and called out for kelp.
Still, something wasn't right about it.
It all smelled fishy to Harry.

Q. Did Harry stay underwater with those odd lifeforms so long on accident?

A. No way, he did it on porpoise!

•

The other day, Moaning Myrtle wasn't feeling too well.
Plus she looked a little flushed.

•

Q. Why did Ron take Hermione out in his flying car?

A. He wanted their relationship to take off.

•

Q. Did you know that the Goblet of Fire used to have a girlfriend?

A. Just an old flame, really.

•

Harry thought about getting brand new glasses and even designing them himself.
But he didn't want to create a spectacle.

Hogwarts requires all its students to be immunized.
With Floo Powder!

•

Q. What's the difference between Ron and Harry, and Fred and George?

A. The first two are roommates, and the other two are womb-mates.

•

Q. What's Professor Lupin's least favorite food?

A. Moon Pies.

•

Q. What's Professor Lupin's favorite Christmas song?

A. "Howl-lejuah."

•

Q. Why did the not-so-smart wizard by a bunch of molds?

A. For *casting* spells.

Whenever McGonagall transformed into a cat she wore galoshes on her feet.

That way she was Puss in Boots!

Q. What's Nearly Headless Nick's favorite drink?

A. Evaporated milk.

•

Q. What should a student never call Professor Snape?

A. Severus!

Q. What should you call the Fat Lady?

A. Um, anything besides "the Fat Lady."

•

Q. Why couldn't Snape teach any more mind-reading classes?

A. The session was at maximum Occlumency.

•

Q. How does Professor Trelawney buy her crystal balls?

A. By the quartz.

•

Q. When is the bread in the Great Hall not bread?

A. When it's a castle-roll.

•

Q. What's the difference between Hagrid and the Mirror of Erised?

A. The mirror is much more polished.

Around Hogwarts

Q. What do you call a hungry Snape?

A. Ravenous Severus.

•

Q. Did you hear that the Hogwarts caretaker was fired for stealing?

A. He tried to "Filch" a book from the restricted section.

•

Harry: What's for dinner today at Hogwarts?

Hermione: Ghoulash, again.

•

Q. What thing at Hogwarts should you never put on your head?

A. The Swording Hat.

•

Snape: Harry, you've got points deducted from Gryffindor five times this week. What do you have to say for yourself?

Harry: TGIF!

Q. Why couldn't Hermione use her Time-Turner?

A. She didn't have time to look for it.

•

Q. What do you call a Hogwarts student who has huge pride for their house?

A. A Slytherin.

•

Malfoy got so mad in Potions class the other day.
He reached his boiling point!

•

There was a Defense Against the Dark Arts class, but no Defense Against the Dark Crafts? What if an evil jewelry box or macaroni-and-glitter painting came along?

•

Professor Trelawney was never out of a job.
She generated a lot of prophets.

Q. How do you get into the gym at Hogwarts?

A. You use the dumbbell-door!

•

Q. How did the artist get into Hogwarts?

A. Draw bridge.

•

Q. Did you know that there's a room at Hogwarts filled with cough drops?

A. It's the Chamber of Sucrets!

•

Q. Did you know there are dogs in the Herbology classroom?

A. Well, there's something in there with bark!

•

Q. How can you tell Professor Sprout's real hair color?

A. Just look for her roots.

Q. What's the Herbology teacher's favorite hip hop band?

A. The Roots!

•

Professor Sprout didn't tolerate fools.
She knew a sap when she saw one.

•

Professor Sprout took great pride in her heritage.
She claims to be related to Leaf Erickson!

•

Q. Why did Professor Sprout need a gardener?

A. Her yard had gone to seed.

•

On the weekends, Professor Sprout just liked to stay home, snuggle up, and weed.

•

Professor Sprout has the dirt on everyone!

94

Q. What's Professor Moody's favorite flower?

A. The Iris.

•

Q. Why did Snape say sad things to a huckleberry potion?

A. He wanted to make it a blueberry potion.

•

Ron: Professor, do you think a person should be punished for something they didn't do?

Snape: I suppose not.

Ron: Good, because I didn't do my Potions homework.

•

When Professor Umbridge took over Hogwarts, it's not that the students hated school—they just didn't like the principal of the thing.

Did you hear that Fred and George turned in the exact same assignment in Muggle Studies about the same car? To be fair, they both had the same car.

•

Fred and George Weasley both flunked their big Herbology final.
They turned in blank papers, although they claim they just used disappearing ink.

•

Professor Binns: Name one notable thing about the wizards of the 17th century.
Ron: They're all dead?

•

Q. Did you hear about the wizard who accidentally drank Veritaserum?
A. It's the truth!

Q. How many Gryffindors does it take to change a light bulb?

A. One, and they win the House Cup for it.

•

Q. Why did so many students want to take Professor Flitwick's class?

A. Because he was so charming!

•

Q. What did they call Myrtle after she read these jokes?

A. Groaning Myrtle!

•

Q. Did you hear that Myrtle gave Hermione five knuts?

A. Good ol' Loaning Myrtle!

•

Q. Did you hear that Dumbledore had some shocking memories?

A. They were extremely o'pensieve!

Q. Why did Dumbledore cross the road?

A. There were lemon drops on the other side!

•

Q. How are your best friends like Oliver Wood?

A. They're keepers!

•

Q. Did you hear Draco was sneaking around Hogwarts after dark?

A. Not really, just Slytherin.

•

Q. How is Hogwarts like the mall?

A. They both have moving staircases!

•

Harry: Why do they call these tests O.W.L.s?

Ron: Because owl certainly fail them.

Around Hogwarts

Q. Who's the worst-written *Harry Potter* character?

A. Nearly Headless Nick . . . because he was poorly executed.

•

Q. Where does Hogwarts get all of its furniture?

A. At Harry Pottery Barn.

•

Q. What's Madame Pomfrey's actual job?

A. She's a witch doctor!

•

Q. Why is Snape named Severus?

A. Because that's what his mother named him.

•

Q. What position will Nearly Headless Nick never achieve?

A. Head Boy.

99

Q. Did you hear about the Hogwarts house with no student supervision?

A. Hey, nobody's prefect.

•

Q. How much does it cost to ride the Hogwarts Express?

A. Nine . . . and three quarters.

Chapter 6

KNOCK-KNOCK-TURN ALLEY

Q. Why can't you tell a Ravenclaw a Knock-Knock Joke?

A. Because if they aren't interested in who's at the door, they won't play along!

•

Knock-knock.
Who's there?
Minerva.
Minerva who?
Minervas . . . to come in, I don't know why!

•

Knock-knock.
Who's there?
Hufflepuff.
Hufflepuff who?
Hufflepuff and I'll blow your house down!

Knock-knock.
Who's there?
Recant.
Recant who?
Recanto my last spell!

•

Knock, knock.
Who's there?
You know.
You know who?
It's okay, he's dead! You can say his name now, silly!

•

Knock-knock.
Who's there?
J.K.
Oh, okay
No . . . knock-knock.
Who's there?
J.K.
Huh?
J.K. Rowling.
Really?
Yes.
I thought you said J.K.?

Knock-Knock-Turn Alley

Knock-knock.
Who's there?
Butterbeer.
Butterbeer who?
Butterbeer around when we need you at D.A. practice!

●

Knock-knock.
Who's there?
Gladys.
Glays who?
Gladys not O.W.L.s time!

●

Knock-knock.
Who's there?
Time-Turner.
Time-Turner who?
Time-Turner us all older and wiser.

Knock-knock.
Who's there?
Icy.
Icy who?
Icy you've got great marks, Luna!

Knock-knock.
Who's there?
Snow.
Snow who?
Snow way we'll find all those horcruxes!

Knock-knock.
Who's there?
Budapest.
Budapest who?
You're nothing Budapest, Rita Skeeter!

Knock-knock.
Who's there?
Butcher.
Butcher who?
Butcher wand away.

Knock-Knock-Turn Alley

Knock-knock.
Who's there?
Fido.
Fido who?
Fido away, will they miss me at Hogwarts?

•

Knock-knock.
Who's there?
Fanny.
Fanny who?
Fanny body calls, I'm studying.

•

Knock-knock.
Who's there?
Gopher.
Gopher who?
Gopher it, the snitch is within reach!

•

Knock-knock.
Who's there?
Gideon.
Gideon who?
Gideon the flying car and let's go to Hogwarts!

Knock-knock.
Who's there?
Nona.
Nona who?
Nona your business, Malfoy!

●

Knock-knock.
Who's there?
Weirdo.
Weirdo who?
Weirdo you think you're going?
Oh no, it's Filch!

●

Knock-knock.
Who's there?
Wanda.
Wanda who?
Wanda when this class will be over?

Knock-Knock-Turn Alley

Knock-knock.
Who's there?
Boo.
Boo who?
It's me, Nearly-Headless Nick, so open up!

●

Knock-knock.
Who's there?
Mimi.
Mimi who?
Mimi at the Room of Requirement!

●

Knock-knock.
Who's there?
Kiwi.
Kiwi who?
Kiwi go to the Quidditch World Cup?

Knock-knock.
Who's there?
Pudding.
Pudding who?
Pudding on your robes before your sweater
is a bad idea.

Knock-knock.
Who's there?
Turnip.
Turnip who?
Turnip the heat, the Ravenclaw common room is so cold!

Knock-knock.
Who's there?
Bean.
Bean who?
Bean to Hogsmeade lately?

Knock-Knock-Turn Alley

Knock-knock.
Who's there?
Pecan.
Pecan who?
Pecan somebody your own size, Crabbe.

●

Knock-knock.
Who's there?
Butternut.
Butternut who?
Butternut go into the restricted section of the library!

●

Knock-knock.
Who's there?
Butter.
Butter who?
Butter bring an umbrella on
our walk to Hagrid's.

Knock-knock.
Who's there?
Raisin.
Raisin who?
Raisin your hand before you speak is how we do things in class.

Knock-knock.
Who's there?
Pizza.
Pizza who?
Pizza candy off the trolley would be great.

Knock-knock.
Who's there?
Omelet.
Omelet who.
Omelet smarter than you think.
We know, Luna.

Knock-Knock-Turn Alley

Knock-knock.
Who's there?
Wafer.
Wafer who?
Wafer the Hogwarts Express, and then you can get on.

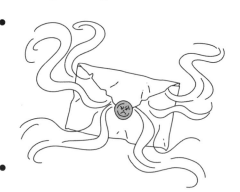

Knock-knock.
Who's there?
Doughnut.
Doughnut who?
Doughnut open that Howler!

Knock-knock.
Who's there?
Curry.
Curry who?
Curry your books to class?

Knock-knock.
Who's there?
Witches.
Witches who?
Witches the right way to Ravenclaw Tower?

•

Knock-knock.
Who's there?
Fang.
Fang who?
Fang you for letting me in!

•

Knock-knock.
Who's there?
Howl.
Howl who?
Howl you know when it's time to leave school?

Knock-Knock-Turn Alley

Knock-knock.
Who's there?
Goblin.
Goblin who?
Goblin your food will make your stomach hurt!

●

Knock-knock.
Who's there?
Boo!
Boo who?
Don't be scared, it's only Peeves!

●

Knock-knock.
Who's there?
Dragon.
Dragon who?
Dragon your robes on the ground, pick
    them up!

113

Knock-knock.
Who's there?
Baby owl.
Baby owl who?
Baby owl see you at the quidditch match?

●

Knock-knock.
Who's there?
Rhino.
Rhino who?
Rhino every spell there is!

●

Knock-knock.
Who's there?
Grr.
Grr who?
Are you Fluffy or an owl?

Knock-Knock-Turn Alley

Knock-knock.
Who's there?
Beavery.
Beavery who?
Beavery quiet under that invisibility cloak!

Knock-knock.
Who's there?
Me.
Me who?
Crookshanks, is that you?

Knock-knock.
Who's there?
Owls.
Owls who?
Of course they do!

Knock-knock.
Who's there?
Detail.
Detail who?
Detail of de thestral is on de end.

Knock-knock.
Who's there?
Garden.
Garden who?
Garden Hogwarts from the Dark Lord!

Knock-knock.
Who's there?
White.
White who?
White in the middle of my homework!

Knock-Knock-Turn Alley

Knock-knock.
Who's there?
Comet.
Comet who?
Comet a crime, go to Azkaban.

•

Knock-knock.
Who's there?
Unit.
Unit who?
Unit me a sweater, Mrs. Weasley?

•

Knock-knock.
Who's there?
Razor.
Razor who?
Razor hand if you know the answer.

•

Knock-knock.
Who's there?
Hallways.
Hallways who?
Hallways late to class!

Knock-knock.
Who's there?
Quill.
Quill who?
Quill we ever meet again?

•

Knock-knock.
Who's there?
Needle.
Needle who?
Needle help with your homework?

•

Knock-knock.
Who's there?
Torch.
Torch who?
Torch you'd never ask!

Knock-Knock-Turn Alley

Knock-knock.
Who's there?
Ginny.
Ginny who?
Ginny a hug!

●

Knock-knock.
Who's there?
Petunia.
Petunia who?
There's a problem Petunia and me.

●

Knock-knock.
Who's there?
Rita.
Rita who?
Rita *Harry Potter* book if you're bored.

Knock-knock.
Who's there?
Arthur.
Arthur who?
Arthur any more Muggle objects around?

•

Knock-knock.
Who's there?
Candy.
Candy who?
Candy mentors even come onto Hogwarts grounds?

•

Knock-knock.
Who's there?
Dewey.
Dewey who?
Dewey or don't we go look for those horcruxes?

Knock-Knock-Turn Alley

Knock-knock.
Who's there?
Grey Lady.
Grey Lady who?
Grey Lady who started
　　Ravenclaw, don't you think?

•

Knock-knock.
Who's there?
Dishes.
Dishes who?
Dishes the end of the chapter?

Chapter 7

LUNA'S LOVELY BEASTS AND MAGICAL CREATURES

Q. How does a dragon say hello?

A. It waves a claw.

Luna's Lovely Beasts and Magical Creatures

Q. How does a basilisk show its appreciation?
A. "Fangs!"

•

Q. Who's Norbert's best friend?
A. Nor-ernie, of course.

•

Q. What did Hagrid get Fluffy for his birthday?
A. Three bones!

Q. Who's a cow's favorite Harry Potter character?

A. Bull Weasley.

•

Q. What can you even say about Peter Pettigrew's crimes?

A. They're unsqueakable!

•

Q. How does a wise and clever eagle say hello?

A. With a wavin' claw!

Q. What's a better name for Fawkes?

A. He who shall not be flamed!

•

Q. What happened when the snake broke the glass at the zoo?

A. A lot of pane!

•

When I say that a griffin is partially a bird, it's only half lion.

125

Dumbledore's phoenix is so smart because he can always out-fawkes people.

●

Q. What *is* the "Order of the Phoenix," anyway?
A. Bird food, or whatever Fawkes would like.

●

People think Fawkes is really smart, even though he's got a bird brain.

●

Q. Why did Fawkes have to leave Hogwarts?
A. He was fired.

●

Q. Fawkes went into Honeydukes and bought some lip balm.
A. He said to put it on his bill.

Q. How did Hagrid weigh Norberta?

A. By her scales.

•

Q. What's Norbert's favorite show?

A. *Claw and Order.*

•

Q. Did you hear Hagrid's dragon lost her tail?

A. Hagrid got a new one at a re-tail store.

•

Q. What do dragons drink out of?

A. Goblets of fire!

•

Q. How is Norbert like Paul Bunyan?

A. Tall tails!

•

Q. What do dragons eat?

A. Anything with hot sauce!

Q. What's the difference between an acromantula and a Dementor?

A. One sucks the life out of its prey . . . and the other is a spider.

•

All the post owls hang out together.
They call it "mail bonding."

•

Hedwig delivered her mail at 4 a.m. once.
Talk about an early bird!

•

Q. Why did Fluffy like camping?

A. He enjoyed ruffing it.

•

Fawkes headed to Gringotts.
He needed some place to deposit his nest egg.

Q. Gringotts employs several rabbits.

A. They're excellent at multiplying.

•

Q. Did you hear that Hedwig was up all night pretending to be a werewolf?

A. She was owling at the moon!

Q. Did you hear that Hedwig had to go to the animal hospital?

A. She needed to be treated for a minor owlment.

•

Q. Why doesn't anyone listen to a mandrake?

A. Because they're blooming idiots!

•

Q. A mandrake went into the Three Broomsticks.

A. It ordered a root beer.

•

Q. What's the opposite of a mandrake?

A. A woman drake!

•

Q. How can you tell if a thestral is about to charge?

A. They take out their credit card.

•

Q. What does a basilisk call a wizard?

A. Dinner!

Q. What kind of books do owls read?
A. Who-dun-its!

•

Q. What was baby Nagini's favorite toy?
A. Her rattle.

•

Q. Why can't centaurs dance?
A. Because they have two left feet!

•

Q. Why do centaurs try to be polite?
A. A tradition of horspitality.

•

Q. What's a centaur's favorite book?
A. *The Call of the Wild.*

•

Q. What did the centaur say when it took a fall?
A. "I've fallen and I can't giddy-up!"

Q. Which side of a centaur has more hair?
A. The outside!

•

Q. There are all those centaurs that live near Hogwarts.
A. What great neigh-bors!

•

Q. Why does nobody take the centaurs seriously?
A. Because they're always horsing around.

•

Hedwig can't seem to remember anybody's names.
She's always saying, "Who?"

•

Q. Why do werewolves have fur coats?
A. They'd look silly in suede ones.

•

Q. How can you tell which end of the basilisk is which?
A. Tickle it in the middle and see which end giggles!

Hermione: I once wrote an essay on the basilisk.
Harry: How did you ever get the typewriter on the basilisk?

•

Q. How do you get fur from an acromantula?
A. Run as fast as you can!

•

If Harry Potter Characters were Chickens
- Clucko Malfoy
- Bellachix
- Cluckshanks
- Bawky Crouch
- Fat Fryer
- Hengrid
- McGonifowl
- Alarooster Moody
- Gilderoy Cluckhart
- Cock-a-Doodle-Dooooby

Q. What's Nagini's favorite game?
A. Swallow the Leader.

•

Q. Why don't owls have tails?
A. So they don't get caught in revolving doors!

•

Q. Why is Buckbeak so big?
A. Because if he was small—and yellow and fuzzy—he'd be a tennis ball!

•

Q. What's long, scaly, and blue?
A. A Hungarian Horntail holding its breath.

•

Q. What did Hagrid feed Fang for breakfast?
A. Pooched eggs.

Q. Why does Fluffy take so long to follow directions?

A. Because it has to process the information three times!

•

Q. Who's a scary werewolf and has a grey back?

A. Fenrir Greyback!

•

Q. Did you hear that Nagini saw a ghost?

A. She jumped right out of her skin!

•

Q. We were going to make a joke about a phoenix here.

A. But it laid an egg.

Chapter 8

COMMON ROOM RIDDLES

Before they can head into the common room and their dorms, Ravenclaws must prove their cleverness by answering a riddle. Riddles like these.

Q. What has hands . . . but cannot clap?

A. A clock.

Q. What must be broken in order to be useful?

A. An egg.

Common Room Riddles

Q. What has one eye but does not see?

A. A needle.

•

Q. A girl sat in her dorm room at night in the dark. No lamp, no torch, no candle. And yet she reads. How?

A. Braille.

•

Q. What lives in winter, dies in summer, and grows with the roots on top?

A. An icicle.

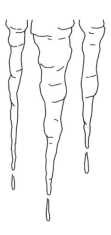

Q. It's been around for millions of years, and yet it's never more than a month old. What is it?

A. The moon.

Q. What word is spelled wrong in every book on earth?

A. Wrong.

Common Room Riddles

Q. It's tall when young and short when it's old. What is it?

A. A candle.

•

Q. What starts with "T," is filled with "T," and then ends in "T?"

A. A teapot.

Q. Throw away the outside, cook the inside, eat the outside, then throw away the inside. What is it?

A. Corn on the cob.

Q. What is full of holes but still holds water?

A. A sponge.

•

Q. What is as light as a feather, but the strongest person in the world couldn't hold it for more than a minute or so.

A. His breath.

•

Q. It has a neck but no head? What is it?

A. A bottle.

•

Q. It's full of keys but can't unlock any door. What is it?

A. A piano.

Common Room Riddles

Q. Two mothers and two daughters went out to a feast. Everyone ate one chicken, yet only three chickens were eaten in all. How is this so?

A. They were a grandmother, a mother, and a daughter.

•

Q. What can run but cannot walk?

A. A drop of water.

•

Q. The one who made it didn't want it, while the one who bought it didn't need it. And the one who used it never even saw it. What is it?

A. A coffin.

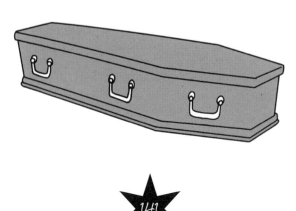

Q. What has a head and a tail but lacks a body?

A. A coin.

●

Q. What occurs once in a minute, but twice in a moment, and *never* in one thousand years?

A. M.

●

Q. What does everyone have but no one can lose?

A. A shadow.

●

Q. What can travel around the world while staying in a corner?

A. A postage stamp.

●

Q. A boy fell off a 20-foot tall ladder, but he did not get hurt. How?

A. He fell off the bottom step.

142

Common Room Riddles

Q. Can you name three consecutive days without saying Wednesday, Friday, and Sunday?

A. Yesterday, today, and tomorrow.

•

Q. What goes up but never comes down?

A. Your age.

Chapter 9

Harry Potter Autocorrect

Here's what our phones did when we tried to text our friends about Harry Potter.

Godric Gryffindor = Goodrich Griffin Did

Helga Hufflepuff = Helps Huddle Puff

Hogsmeade = Hogshead

Zonko's = So Kid

Honeyduke's = Honey Dukedom

Diagon Alley = Saigon Alley

Eelops = Ellipsis

Ollivander's = Olive Derby

Beauxbatons = Beau Barons

Durmstrang = Fur Strange

Dementors = Deme Today

Rubeus Hagrid = Rubies Harris

Albus Dumbledore = Album Dumb Direction

Severus Snape = Several Snapshots

Umbridge = Unbridgeable

Remus Lupin = Remission Lupine

Expecto Wordplay!

Flitwick = Felt Wicker
Minerva McGonagall = Minor Said MC Gonna
Hermione = Her Minor
Draco Malfoy = Dragon Malformed
Neville Longbottom = Never Long Board
Percy Weasley = Percussion Weasel Your
Goyle = Gould
Crabbe = Crane
Hedwig = He'd Wiggle
Igor Karkaroff = Igor Karma Riff
Peeves = Perverse
Crookshanks = Crooks Hanks
Buckbeak = Buck Brakes
Dobby = Donuts
Luna Lovegood = Lunar Love Goodbye
Fleur Delacour = Flyer Deals Our
Bellatrix Lestrange = Bells Tricks Lest Rangers
Srimgeour = Scrim Grout
Bathilda Bagshot = Bath Island Bags Hot
Quirrell = Quit Telling
Aberforth Dumbledore = Abercrombie Dumble Direction

Harry Potter Anagram quiz

Can you guess what these Harry Potter *abbreviations* really *stand for?*

1. N.E.W.T.
   a. Neville Eventually Will Try
   b. Nobody Ever Write-Off Trelawney
   c. Nastily Exhausting Wizarding Tests

2. S.P.E.W.
   a. Some Potions Eerily Whisper
   b. Scabbers Probably Eats Wigs
   c. Society for the Promotion of Elfish Welfare

3. O.W.L.
   a. Occlumency Will Liberate
   b. Oh, Wow Luna!
   c. Ordinary Wizarding Levels

4. D.A.
   a. Don't Apparate!
   b. Dumbledore's Armpit
   c. Dumbledore's Army

146

5. J.K. Rowling
   a. Just Knuts
   b. James Krum
   c. Joanne (and the "k" doesn't represent anything)

Answers: All "c."

•

Wizarding Tom Swifties

"The number of people not attending class today really bothers me," said Professor Snape, absent-mindedly.

"Your aunt is coming," Vernon guessed.

"House elves must have done it!" Draco implied.

"I hope you're not afraid of needles," Madame Pomfrey injected.

"I prefer weirder common room entry paintings," said Luna abstractly.

"I just got a job putting up the quidditch goals!" Colin Creevey beamed.

"I am not full of hot air!" Harry's aunt belched.

"I need to sharpen this sword of Gryffindor," said Neville bluntly.

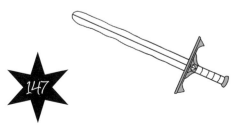

"I'll go get the Elder Wand," said Voldemort fetchingly.

"I fixed the toilet," announced Filch, flushed with success.

"I will not finish in fifth place," Viktor held forth.

"That goblet is on fire!" yelled Dumbledore alarmingly.

"We've taken over Hogwarts," the Death Eater cooed.

"Yes, I'm that strongly built," said Cedric soberly.

"I wrote the book on that subject," said Gilderoy authoritatively.

"I designate Harry as my chief heir," said Sirius willingly.

"The fire in the common room is going out!" Luna bellowed.

"I think I'll use a different font on this assignment," said Hermione boldly.

"The mirror of Erised!" Harry reflected.

"There's room in the D.A. for one more," Harry admitted.

"Weasley is our king!" the Gryffindors said cheerfully.

"Padfoot is my godfather," said Harry in all seriousness.

"You can't even look after my plants while I'm away," said Professor Sprout witheringly.

"One lump or two?" asked Professor Umbridge sweetly.

"I work at a bank," said Griphook tellingly.

148

Expecto Wordplay!

"Here's your homework for the next two weeks," Professor McGonagall advanced.

"That painting makes me laugh," Neville articulated.

"I'm going to get a hair transplant," said Voldemort baldly.

"Azkaban is a necessary evil, I think," said Dumbledore cagily.

"This pudding is only 50% set," Ron affirmed.

"Gringotts doesn't even want me as a depositor," said Tonks unaccountably.

"Want a chocolate frog?" Ron croaked.

"The wand fell apart in my hands," Harry rejoined.

"I want to date other guys," said Lavender unsteadily.

"Take the Marauder's Map and you'll never get lost," said the pathologist.

"Pettigrew, you're of greater value to me every day," said Voldemort appreciatively.

"We had to camp the entire time we searched for horcruxes," said Hermione very attentively.

"I hate climbing this winding staircase," said the Ravenclaw coyly.

"Tea, Mr. Potter?" asked Professor McGonagall briskly.

"Use your own hair brush!" Hermione bristled.

"That wizard did a bad job," said Hagrid disenchantedly.

"Let's visit the cemetery in Godric's Hollow," said Harry gravely.

"I teach here," Flitwick professed.

"Okay, you can borrow it again, Hermione," the librarian relented.

"I'm under the sorting hat," said Luna off the top of her head.

"Long ago, a werewolf bit me," said Lupin rabidly.

"All I ever do is work," Ron droned.

"This boat to Hogwarts leaks," said Hermione balefully.

"Can you get me out of Azkaban soon?" asked Sirius balefully.

"I'm going back to school soon," said Luna with class.

Expecto Wordplay!

"I was removed from office," said the Minister of Magic disappointedly.

"This must be the Hogwarts gym," Hermione worked out.

"I find you guilty!" said Professor Umbridge with conviction.

"I floated from the Great Hall to here," said Nearly Headless Nick, visibly moved.

"Wand battles hurt my hands," said Cho callously.

"Take me to the Yule Bawl!" the Hufflepuff bawled.

"You are going to fail my class," said Professor Snape, degradingly.

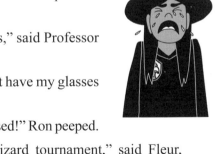

"The optician probably doesn't have my glasses ready," Harry speculated.

"I looked into the Mirror of Erised!" Ron peeped.

"I came in third in the Triwizard tournament," said Fleur, meddlingly.

"Professor Trelawney isn't the best medium," Hermione said dispiritedly.

"I'm going to hypnotize you now, mom," said Hermione transparently.

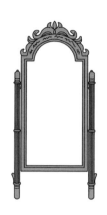

"Ah, I've just been stabbed with a sword!" said Nagini pointedly.

"Oh, goody! Another blackout!" said Ginny delightedly.

"I got hurt playing quidditch," said Oliver Wood disjointedly.

•

Riddles!

A wizarding legend from back in the day
To save Draco, with my life I did pay.
Who am I?
Professor Dumbledore

•

I turn into a cat for fun
When I don't have Gryffindor to run.
Who am I?
Professor McGonagall

Expecto Wordplay!

The Marauders thought I was weak
But I'm actually a spy. Squeak-squeak!
Who am I?
Peter Pettigrew, a.k.a. Scabbers

•

I live near the school in a hut
And I'm a half giant. So what?
Who am I?
Rubeus Hagrid

•

What ended my life?
Lestrange's thrown knife!
Who am I?
Dobby

•

Perhaps I am telling too soon
My secret: I howl at the moon!
Who am I?
Remus Lupin

To other wizards I bring bad will
Because of what I write with my quill.
Who am I?
Rita Skeeter

•

Harry asked me to the Yule Ball too late
Because Cedric was already my date.
Who am I?
Cho Chang

•

I might be a world-class seeker
But I have trouble as a comfortable speaker.
Who am I?
Viktor Krum

•

I served to be Harry's foil
Oh, look, here come Crabbe and Goyle.
Who am I?
Draco Malfoy

Expecto Wordplay!

At Hogwarts my plans were undone
Because two heads were in place of my one.
Who am I?
Professor Quirrell

•

In an important duel did I fail
And sadly I went through the veil.
Who am I?
Sirius Black

•

I'm related to Sirius Black
But that doesn't mean I have his back.
Who am I?
Bellatrix Lestrange

•

I don't care for non-magical breeds
And I'll punish until your hand bleeds.
Who am I?
Professor Umbridge

I killed Dumbledore, how sad?
But through it all, I wasn't so bad.
Who am I?
Professor Snape

•

The other side blew off my ear
But hey, at least I'm still here.
Who am I?
George Weasley

•

They say that I'm silly, that's true.
Now, has anyone seen my left shoe?
Who am I?
Luna Lovegood

•

I opened the Chamber of Secrets
And then married Potter, no regrets!
Who am I?
Ginny Weasley

Expecto Wordplay!

My witching abilities are keen
Thanks to my library trips being routine.
Who am I?
Hermione Granger

•

My hair is the brightest of red
Without me, Harry would likely be dead.
Who am I?
Ron Weasley

•

The embodiment of evil? That's me!
But I was thwarted by just a baby!
Who am I?
Lord Voldemort

•

The most notable wizard in the biz
They wrote seven books about me, gee whiz!
Who am I?
Harry Potter

Chapter 10

THIS IS RIDDIKULUS!

Q. What do wizards wear on their feet?

A. Sneakerscopes.

•

Q. What's the difference between Ron Weasley and a magic wand?

A. One is a person and the other is an enchanted object.

•

Q. What's dark, scary, and full of *American Idol* hosts?

A. The Chamber of Seacrest.

•

Q. Have you heard the one about Dungbombs?

A. It stinks!

This is Riddikulus!

Q. How come Dobby didn't want to give up his sock?
A. Because he was very elfish!

•

When actual wizards watch a magic show, is that like when professional rock musicians see somebody play *Guitar Hero*?

•

Q. Where would you find Floo Powder?
A. On the Floo(r).

•

Q. What do wizards do on Halloween?
A. They drink a vial of Polyjuice Potion!

•

Fake Harry Potter Spoilers to tell Your Muggle Friends
- Snape is Harry's dad.
- Harry dies at the end.
- Dumbledore and Ron are the same person.
- Hermione was a ghost all along.

159

- Hagrid was controlling Voldemort.
- Nobody can really do magic—they're just pretending.
- Dumbledore kills McGonagall.
- Hedwig becomes the Minister of Magic.
- Hogwarts is saved at the last minute by a new student named K.J. Rowling.

●

Q. Are you a wizard?
A. No, I just like wearing a cape to school for no reason.

●

Q. Is that a magic wand?
A. No, it's just a stick I found that shoots green energy beams.

●

Q: Does it hurt when the Skele-Gro regrows your bones?
A: No, it's exactly like drinking a Butterbeer.

This is Riddikulus!

Q: Did you unlock that door with magic?
A: No, I'm psychic and I did it with my mind.

•

Q. Did you hear that Harry got that flying contraption Ron stole, and got it fixed up and safely drove it for years?
A. Harry's car never bothered him again.

•

Q. Did you hear that Voldemort's car got a flat tire and he got stranded in the middle of nowhere?
A. He'd killed the spare.

•

Q. What's another name for the *Fantastic Beasts* movies?
A. *Barely Potter.*

•

New wizard board game: *Hungry Hungry Hippogriffs.*

Q. How is wizard *Monopoly* different from regular *Monopoly*?

A. You "go directly to Azkaban."

•

Q. How is wizard *Operation* different from regular *Operation*?

A. You just fix the patient with Skele-Gro.

•

Q. What happened when Voldemort played *The Game of Life*?

A. He left chunks of his game piece all over the board.

•

Q. What's the difference between Dumbledore and J.K. Rowling?

A. Rowling owns her own castle.

This is Riddikulus!

Things About Harry Potter That Still Don't Make Sense to Us

- Why is the house animal of Ravenclaw an eagle and not a raven?
- How come people aren't using the Time-Turner constantly?
- How are there only four wizard schools in the entire world?
- Why does Voldemort always wait until spring to execute each attack on Harry?
- How does nobody notice "Moody" drinking Polyjuice Potion all the time?
- Harry names his kid after "the bravest men I know" but his name isn't Ron?
- The Remembrall tells you that you've forgotten *something,* but not *what* you've forgotten. Which kind of defeats the purpose.
- The only muggles aware of magic are . . . the Dursleys?
- Why do parents keep sending their kids to this dangerous school?
- Nobody *ever* saw rat-form Peter Pettigrew on the Marauder's Map?
- How can Voldemort lead the pureblood revolution when he himself is a "half-blood"?

- Harry should have been able to see the thestrals all along, as he knew death.
- Why does Harry need glasses? Can't he magically fix his eyesight?

•

Q: "Ash" me what my wand is made of.
Okay, what's your wand made of?
Ash.
Okay, what's your wand made of?
Ash!
I am!

•

The Most Magical Places in the U.S.A.
- Wichita
- San Francodraco
- Dumbledoregon
- McGonagallabama
- Diggoreno

This is Riddikulus!

Q. What's a wizard's favorite old movie?
A. *Gone With the Wand.*

•

Q. What's the ooziest place?
A. The Chamber of Secretions.

•

Hagrid: You're an electric wizard, Harry!
Harry: Watt?

•

Q. Why did Harry leave the Dursleys with regret?
A. He regretted having to live there at all!

•

Q. What does the Whomping Willow drink?
A. Root beer.

•

Q. Why couldn't Harry drink butterbeer?
A. It kept falling out of his glasses.

165

Q. How do you confuse a wizard?

A. Paint yourself purple and throw a spoon at her.

•

Q. What did the wizard say to the other wizards?

A. "We're wizards!"

•

Q. What do you call a wizard on the moon?

A. An astronaut that can do magic!

This is Riddikulus!

Q. What do you call a wizard from space?
A. A flying sorcerer.

•

Q. What did the wizard say when he lost his wand?
A. "Where's my wand?"

•

Q. Why isn't Nicolas Flamel a good wizard?
A. Because he died decades ago.

•

Q. Why wasn't the wizard bald?
A. Because he was Harry.

•

Q. What's a dog's favorite Harry Potter book?
A. *Hairy Pawter and the Deathly Howls.*

Q. What do you call a witch on an iceberg?
A. A cold spell.

Q. What amazing thing happened to Harry on his 12th birthday?
A. He wasn't 11 anymore.

This is Riddikulus!

Q. In what states would you be most likely to find Dementors?

A. North and South Scarolina.

•

Q. What's scarier than one Dementor?

A. Five Dementors!

•

How to Know You're a Potterhead

You ask every cat you see if they're Professor McGonagall.

You ask every dog you see if they're Sirius.

You don't trust rats. *Ever.*

You try to free classmates from school by giving them socks.

You think a Time-Turner triggers Daylight Saving Time.

•

Q. What kind of pizza do wizards like?

A. Pepperoni and Ollivanders.

Q. What wand would your grandparents choose?

A. The Elder Wand.

Q. What do you get when you combine winter weather with Beauxbatons?

A. Snow Fleur-ies!

•

Q. What toy do young wizards and witches watch at Christmas?

A. The House Elf on the Shelf.

This is Riddikulus!

Q. What's the biggest elf in the world?
A. A house elf—they're the size of a house!

•

Q. Where do wizards go to watch other wizards play video games?
A. Witch Twitch.

•

Q. What's the difference between a ghost and Peter Pettigrew?
A. One is a phantom, and the other is a fan o' Tom.

•

Here's a picture of an invisibility cloak: